INTO

THE

DEEP BLUE

DAVIDSON REHAM

COPYRIGHT

Into The Deep Blue: A Lesson of Life & Love by Davidson Reham

Published by Davidson Reham

www.infinerotech.com

Copyright © 2022 Davidson Reham

Cover by Infinero Technology

Other supporters and participation by: The Rise of the Golden Stars, The Okonjo radio station, Infinero Technology and J.E.D Poetry.

To buy books by this author,Visit

https://kdp.amazon.com

Signup and get access

to unlimited books

AUTHOR'S MESSAGE AND DEDICATION

I'm immensely grateful that this book is in your hands. My deep hope is that it accomplishes the full purpose of helping you understand the importance of love to life and cultivating that quality to ensure better relationships in every facet of your daily life.

Into The Deep Blue is based on the concept and principle that has shaped my life to simplicity and happiness. It highlights the importance and depth of the simple quality – love, connecting its truth to the experience of exploring different shades of blue.

I have given most of what I have to give in the writing of this book for you and I thank all the good people from around the world who have stood with me all through my journey of discovery and creativity.

My parents who inspired me to higher ideas of life, for their prayers, sacrifices, and their endless patience - they are "Heaven on Earth" for me.

My family: Runyi Chuks, Progress Reham, Divine-Treasure Michael - my helper, inspiration, supporter, fan and friend.

Taylor Alison Swift, whose music helped me towards dark times and depression, and brought out a better version of me towards creativity and love.

I dedicate this book to all those mentioned and to everyone reading this book – thank you and I hope you enjoy the book.

Contents

Epigraph

In a world where life is a journey, let love lead, for lovers long for the time their soul may blend in a whisper.

CHAPTER ONE

(Mind Of A Poet)

A Letter To Stress

O ye world Giant!!!

Like a plug you are plugged

in lives of all humans

without a visible connection.

From the big to the small,

from the old to the young,

you have made no partiality

as your impact is catastrophic.

Your blow is as mighty as thunder

and you set more reputation for yourself

than others.

In pain you do thread

and more pain you afflict.

For you walk in broken hearts,

to deadly illnesses,

from competition to strife,

from high expectations to disgrace,

from love to regrets and shame.

For your pleasure is pain

and more pain is your treasure.

How I would love

To comprehend your concept,

but no!

You're a mystery,

and you're being treated with contempt.

Your jealousy is outstanding

for no one notices your absence,

so you make yourself known withstanding.

Like a snail you crawl,

but you manifest like a giant

and prey on exhausted souls of high hopes.

Little does a man know your worth.

For if you're a person,

you will be worshipped,

lest your wrath not befall us all.

So here I write you oh world giant,

in your mercy, may we thread

for in health, may we not sly

may your absence bring us happiness

and peacefully may we sleep

to a gentle lullaby.

Mind Of A Poet

On a bright dark night,

behold a dreamer.

With dazzling eyes

gazing at naked nature.

Watching the leaves of the trees

dance to the rhythm of the wind,

a thousand thoughts creeps his mind

as he stares into the sky in plain sight.

Of what shall become a human

when humanity is lost?

Will my life be gone together with

the foretold generational curse?

Should I die today,

can I bid farewell without knowing real love?

My answers I wish to find above.

For there are a million minds

in my single mind

many in doubts,

many in fear

as I let my emotions

walk as words,

my inner demons

make me work.

Twisted are my thoughts

of a strange paradigm

sorry to the one

who tries to understand.

They can be of love,

they can be of hate,

here is a welcome

to the mind of a poet.

CHAPTER TWO

(Love Genesis)

I Saw You

My eyes almost fell from looking at you,

I did not just see you – I saw you!

Behind the smile and giggles

lies a girl desiring to be free

I fell in love, for you were like me.

Sweaty palms, I hesitated

and my first approach was not physical.

Lots of text revealed ourselves,

we grew closer before we met.

You are a fine treasure of something divine

a perfect jewel I can't describe.

Your history I came to know wasn't a shock,

from the beginning I was sure

for I did not just see you – I saw you.

That Day, I Fell In Love

Your warm welcoming hands

on my waist on a Wednesday afternoon,

made me weary to the wobbling thoughts

of escaping your wonderful touch of cool.

As I looked into your eyes

of alluring desires,

lies loyalty and a lifetime

of lovely alliance.

I was lost in you, and in you I felt lust.

For you wiped my tears

and whispered to my ears

a sentence of unswerving hope,

my spirit went above

and in that day, I fell in love.

Teenage Emotions

Am I going crazy?

Or did I just forget to stay sane?

Of all the troubles,

do I just want to feel pain?

But these feelings are far from pain.

They are curious,

craving the answer

to a mysterious adventure.

Is this a forever thing?

Or will I wish to die at the end?

When the feelings are gone

Will I love myself instead?

Butterflies in my stomach

and a memory bed,

one I lie in to travel

to a romantic realm.

If this smile is my happy place,

then here I'll stay

throughout my days.

Blessed am I

to find the whole package

that stirs up emotions

I can't manage.

They said it's bad,

they said it's dangerous,

but I can't find anyone

who's more humorous.

So innocent and feeble

are what people consider harmful

yet I fall to a dangerous space.

Is it early to feel this way?

Yes!

But do I have a strong reason to?

Many is a word rarely used

to find that one who commits you.

I may be lost in your eyes

but I've never been more found.

And though my emotions are teenagery,

it is a natural human feeling.

Lifestyle

It smells, it spreads,

you can't hide it,

For it is here.

It is everywhere.

And visible not to the eyes,

but to the mind.

It is shown

when you live it for a while.

A concept

many are yet to understand,

but important

as it is to life.

For who you are

reflects in your actions,

and your actions

speaks your mind.

Take me away

with deep questions of life

that my lifestyle may be simple and mild.

If I should join Davy Jones tonight,

will I live on in people's mind?

For my lifestyle

is ruled by love

that walks in plain sight

in my acquaintances minds.

With natural affection

shall I taste too sweet

that I may seek peace

with whomever I'm seen with

Of what life I lived

if I'm not remembered?

I fear I live in vain

of wasteful encounters.

For a life of love is fully lived

far it spreads to every facet

of a complete human being.

In general, it thrives

in romantic relationships,

and friendships,

neighborhoods and acquaintances,

but a lifestyle begins with family.

Family may tell the tales

of a beloved son.

A son that makes sacrifices

to ensure survival.

A son that put himself last

on daily intervals.

A son that can be a father,

peace to the home he fuels.

A son that can also be a girl.

For there are no gender discrimination

in sharing love.

Everyone accounts

for their self-made ploy.

But if good reputations

are based on love,

then create a lifestyle

that shows what you stand for.

If Love Was a Person

If love was a person

I'll be a girl,

calm as the wind

when the daylight fades,

beautiful in person

as each day passes by,

if love was a person.

If love was a person

I'll be a witch,

charming every person

that dares fall for me,

raining curses on every

fellow with wrong motives,

if love was a person.

If love was a person

I'll wed the sincere,

spread my arms open

to a very simple pearl,

building a family

of the me that I felt,

if love was a person.

Can't you see

it is as simple as a scene,

it must have been the way

you perceived it.

If for a fact,

you see it crystal clear

then love can be a person.

If love was a person

I'll be a mother,

bringing forth children

that human acquires,

sacrificing my lot

and temporal power,

if love was a person.

If love was a person

I'll be a healer,

healing all the scars

that I inflicted on you,

pushing you further

to a happier truth,

if love was a person.

Can't you feel the atmosphere

whenever I'm around you?

It is definitely the way

that I see you.

If your life is as simple and complete,

then you've met love in person.

No matter who you are,

you've met love in person.

Make Believe

Once upon a poem

Is the start of my wild adventure

as trouble met my gaze

looking like outright pleasure.

It was sad and beautiful

like a nurtured emotion.

In my head was a boat created

taking me to a different dimension

creating fantasies

as I fantasize in my imagination

where love was a person

with clear intentions.

I hold unto thee

with high expectations

screaming and clearing my path.

Yes! My path to a fairytale

where I long to live long

without looking pale,

where my language of love

is spoken with strong faith,

where I wish to die

to live again,

where I sing a song

of happy days.

But to life I know

is a funny joke.

My tale of love

won't last that long.

It longs to see me plan and hope

just to crush my tender soul.

Tell me how to face this reality

as life plays games of make believe.

If in loss, life should bring me ecstasy,

then I'll make believe my reality.

Infant Infatuation

Who will save me

from this temporary sly?

Though his days are numbered

he still put up a fight.

He gets you lost

only to lust for a while

and then he leaves

to leave you with a scar.

My fragile heart bleeds

expectations of a coming sad feeling,

one I don't understand to be

If I'm to be more reasoning.

It ignites my being

to a whole new chapter

of a story, it's ending

I won't want to believe.

Fly far away from me

you narcissistic demon!

Something I wish not say

to your colorful nature.

It's difficult to say no to you

for just as I want you to go

I still crave your truth.

Yes! Save me please

save me

he is determined to enslave me.

but don't go

make me feel better

I just want you to last forever.

Very early did you inspire

emotions in me

I never wish to acquire.

And if many wonder

what be your mission,

you were born to me

as my infatuation.

Always and Forever (Part 1)

You must have heard stories

of a certain phrase:

"Always and forever" to a fairytale.

Always contains tragic event

and a happy end

to bring you comfort

on a certain trend.

But you give to me real love

A love so eager to show off,

A love that makes it difficult

to give up,

A love that sprung

from Infatuation

That I saw you

for the first time

at your window

with a wide smile,

I took a step

I never knew will change my life.

That certain day

at your grand dad's house,

was one too many

in my mother's arms.

You showed me comfort and love

infatuation became jealous.

That I was attracted to you

is false

I was drawn to your adventure.

This feeling is sincere

of a much greater mission than pleasure.

I wonder what our tragedy might be

for the love we share

is not forbidden.

Strong as the tide,

shocking like light's current,

this love speaks to me

in ocean's torrent.

For today I swear to you,

by my side

you will always be,

your happiness

will be my reason to live,

you will be

to me, my helper,

and I will love you

Always and Forever.

CHAPTER THREE

(Reality)

Love and Deception

I said I love you

but I lied.

I said you were one In a million

but the truth is

you were one among millions.

Yes you bloom

indeed you rose,

you were human

not to mention your pose.

We were actors in disguise

but you performed

well for the crowd

and I smiled

for you didn't know

I was a director

among the crowd

and I knew better.

Looking deep in your eyes

is all it took to know your world.

You fell in my charming eyes

as I kicked in your heart.

Oh! I wonder how deep

you fell for me!!!

I knew you and your treachery

but I rode on for I wasn't excluded

in our mutual ride of brilliant lies.

Like shadows in darkness

was our intentions hidden

for in pretense we harness

love that was forbidden.

So many times could I pull out

but I was drowning in your pitiful ply

and as I watch you win and dominate

I kept awaiting my prince charming

to come by.

You wanted my physical

and I want a future

that is why what we had

was not something to nurture.

I won't forget you

for you made my history.

And in later years I'll relate

this sad beautiful tragic!

What If

What if we start over

from the beginning?

No flaws, no fights

Just a life of meaning.

What if you don't feel guilty

and my heart is as strong as stone

like a good foundation building?

What if we never met

and I didn't fall for love

will I still cry to sleep every night

to prove a point?

What if I had a name

of a more specific reputation

will I earn more respect

and my salvation?

What if I never had stepped out that Friday

and I stayed indoors on that Monday

will my life be more simple

and my conscience more mild?

What if I am not paranoid

and I'm just like every other person

will I find peace and confidence?

What if I didn't collide with my mum's eggs

and I wasn't formed,

will I be less of a burden

to the world and it's norms?

What if I wasn't writing this poem

will my feelings still hurt

and my spirit slip slowly

to a more distant realm?

What if there are no what if's

and I never fell for less

then I guess I wouldn't

have written a letter to stress.

The Deep Blue

A long gaze

at different shades of colors

will bring to life

certain prospects of reality.

As I make my home blue

to tell a story

of my experience,

feelings of nostalgia

hugged my skinny body.

There are shades of blue

that tells different stories.

Many are languages

yet to be understood.

When you look closely

to life's phases

certain colors parades your eyes

but this time

we talk of blue.

Life is a simple complication

if studied brings

inner peace and comfort.

For what you need in life is love

A fact, long ago

I wish I knew

and in translation

love as we know it

gives feelings of blue.

But love is rarely shown

it is mostly misunderstood.

Two sides of a coin

that breaks relationships

without giving a clue.

For we know

only the surface

and we wish for it

to end there,

but love elongates

its legs further, sadly to despair.

To try you

and play games with you

not for boredom

but to ensure you're sincere

and if there are weaknesses

it will leave you for dead.

Blue is important in every

phase of life

but she hides herself

behind the pure at hearts.

For just as different

shades reveals her strength,

so does love test your patience.

It is deeper than you think,

it is a journey

to the end of the world.

You will encounter various phases

before arriving at your point.

Many will be frightening,

and the good times are few

but at the end

you will achieve your muse.

So before leaving

ask an important question,

are you ready

for a journey

into the deep blue?

Family Ties

Family is sacred

it's not about blood

it's who's reaching for you

when you're drowning in mud

when life drags you down

and you have no strength to stand

it is family who'd die

pulling you from the sand

it is memories and moments

 it is lives intertwined

and who knows your soul

keeps you in your right mind.

To spit on that bond

like it was nothing

says more about you

and that's saying something.

You really should think

while you're on that ledge

about who's going to catch you

when you fall off the edge.

Because bloody and broken

is not a good look

you might want to rethink

the step you just took.

About what family means

when it's written in stone

about dying together

and dying alone.

I promise they're different

than words can portray

I hope that you are hearing

the words that I say.

No bond is eternal,

for all can be broken

by something as simple

as words left unspoken.

The lines that you're crossing

are doors that can close

locking behind you

leaving you cold.

When they've had enough

of the blood that they shed

freely for you

while you left them for dead.

I see it all coming

from way over here,

family is not nothing

it can disappear.

Love & War

Take that eyes off me

your sight disgusts me

but I don't want to see

you talking to another man.

Stay where I want you to

embrace me dearly

but your touch on my body

make me want to puke.

You are not

what I thought you were

you deceived me

there are many men

I could have fallen for

but I fell for your lies

and you used me.

You are not half a man

and I don't want your hands on me

you can't even satisfy

A lady sexually.

Of what use are you

to me as a woman?

Your nails are more important

to you than my stomach.

If for a fact

you worked hard enough

to provide

then you will have enough

to eat when you get back.

But you are as lazy

as my grandmother

when she was eighty.

Go to the ants

and you'll get

some insights maybe.

That's all you do,

run your mouth

and challenge my authority.

No respect, no submission

no priority.

I have my flaws

I agree but I adore you,

yet you have your eyes

fixed on a fantasy

that won't come true.

Speak when you're a woman

when you have needs to meet,

A visitor every month

and my skin upkeep.

You will want to

show your wife off

to all of your friends,

but you won't want to

pay the bill when it

comes in the end.

Accept your responsibility

and I will be proud,

I will sing your praises

to everyone in the crowd.

But no! you prefer

you stay at home every day,

making calls to little girls

you met at the subway.

Yes I make those calls

and I feel at ease

because in my house

living rent free is conflict.

That's what happens

when you have a nagging wife

when all she does

is find fault and

mess up your whole life.

Your mouth will push all

your loved ones away someday

you're just like your mother

you never watch what you say.

I should have known

when I saw

how you treated your family

it will come back and bite me

if I make you family.

I wonder what I felt…

I wondered what I felt too!

To think that someone

like you could make my happy muse.

You worth nothing to me

I'm just mad I got used

but of all, I'm glad

I never had a baby with you.

I'm gone!!!

Marriage Misconception

I wish I never met him.

I wish I never met her.

Words of regrets

walks their path.

The bigger picture

they wish they saw

but the main picture

they didn't see

What shall be my next step?

Dangerous questions

crawls their heart

and dangerous advice

they seek to find.

For what they are looking

they already crave

they just want to hear It

from someone else's cave.

For the heart is treacherous

Who can know it?

But advices are given

from a different perspective.

They put it to work

in their own experience

it yields different result

and they blame it on their partner

at their marriage expense.

Mistakes too little

brings down a strong tower

so does misconceptions

reduces marriage's power.

For lack of patience is shown

and assumptions are preserved

that will lead to conclusions

of a totally wrong design.

At the end of the day,

they both will resign.

Breaking Point

Hope is a dangerous thing

and endurance is futile.

I have waited a million years

for a different person

to sprout from the same

person I know.

Who am I deceiving?

An apple tree only brings forth apple

so why expect otherwise?

There is a thin line

between giving a chance

and being a fool.

A fool

I wish not to be.

If that will change my being

I shall decide it to be.

For my lessons have been

learned the hard way

and I will be a fool

should I not believe.

A decision I have made

and I believe

will bring me peace.

For love was made

to be a good thing

but at the end of the day

I am leaving.

Without Warning

I walked into your life

proudly with joy outstanding.

I found a home

as I watched you two grow,

I felt safe

that I will last to the end.

But sadly you took me

off without warning.

What shall I say to the next couple I meet?

Will I trust them to accept me forever?

For as you're broken

did you break me

and you both couldn't

stand the test of time.

You begged for my presence,

and I showed myself to you.

You went down the deep blue

but you came out confused.

What shall I say to myself

now that I am lonely?

As you looked in my eyes

and pushed without warning.

CHAPTER FOUR

(Lessons Learned)

Take Me Back (Part 1)

Take me back!

Please take me back.

Take me back to days of old,

days of medieval,

when honor was the code,

and nobility the currency.

When loyalty was held

at high esteem.

When air was made,

from nature's steam.

Take me back to principles,

when manners were modest cup

dipped in deep waters,

of fine conduct.

When a man's word

was a honest oath,

and i could feel confident

in my confidant.

Take me back

to days of kings

days of earls,

and the marquees.

When a Viscount speak

with silent sound,

when reputation

was in men's heart.

oh! how i love the English,

for in culture did they soar,

with respect,

did they bless their rules,

an enigma

of moral excellence.

But,

now i look around

and weep,

that humanity

as whole bleeds.

Had recent men

been like past times,

then my tale of old

won't be this bold!

Take Me Back (Part 2)

Take me back!

Please take me back!

Take me back to the woman's world,

the times before this generation called,

before proper mentality was sold

the times before

the women's curse bestowed.

Take me back to reasoning,

when a woman's words

were seasoning.

When her thoughts

were filled with wisdom

when her conversations

can build a man of vision.

Take me back to modest fashion,

when women adorn themselves

with caution

when the modiste produce

dresses of decent designs,

when lust was rare

in a woman's eyes.

Take me back to chastity,

when a woman's pride

was her virginity,

when in deep stares,

affection were shown

when an unmarried man

and woman can't be alone.

Take me back

to her youthful plight,

when her longing

was to be a man's wife.

And she brags,

not against him but in him

that she accomplished her purpose

as a woman indeed.

Yet in women I lost hope,

for they became bold

and got lost in their heart desires.

If only they can walk in their past fame,

then the woman's world

could be born again.

Take Me Back (Part 3)

Take me back!

Please take me back!

Take me back to an ancient union,

the day when a man and a woman become one,

the day their parent side,

they decide to leave,

the day love paid a visit in public.

Take me back to their wedding night,

firecrackers and a sorrowful bye

when they see themselves fully

for the first time,

and wait nine months

to show the world

their wedding right.

Take me back

to when they knew their right

when their parents don't have to interfere

in their every fight.

Far away they go

to make their new home

of love, creating lives and building hope.

~ 65 ~

Take me back

to when they shared chores

when a husband speaks

with authority and love

when absolute submission

was a wife's breath

and deep respect was

her closest friend.

There did she know her place,

under her husband's headship

did she feel safe

and like an infant in the mother's arm

does the husband protect her

as he does his life.

So why the vast difference in this age?

for competitions

are what recent couple face

couples with couple fights

gives couples discoloring phase

which makes a movie last

than most marriages today.

Take Me Back (Part 4)

Take me back!

Please take me back!!!

Take me back to weighty responsibilities

life in the hands

of two imperfect beings.

In their home they heard

their very own infant cry

driving silence far a distant realm.

Take me back to parenthood,

where a child has its original root.

when DNA wasn't public knowledge

but every parent knows

their child by blood.

Take me back

to a parent's task,

when they knew the true value of life

that death wasn't created

for an unborn child

and a bastard was still,

shamefully theirs.

Take me back

to spoken instructions,

when parents strive

to inculcate sound visions

values of deep intimate moral standings

tied with love

and spiritual tidings.

Take me back

to a father's love,

when he wakes up with eagerness

to take his oldest son to work,

when family becomes a priority

than his preferential choice,

when he kisses his daughter's forehead

every night to indicate love.

Take me back to a mother's life,

when she only live

to protect her child,

when sacrifices were her daily footsteps

made without a second thought

to ensure her children's future.

Take me back

as i cry out loud,

parents are not who you think they are.

They are super humans

with an imperfect life

drinking sweats to make you feel alive.

If from their responsibilities

they stray today,

their burden i understand

brings pain,

but couples today

should really know this sort

it's either you're a parent,

or you're not.

Take Me Back (Part 5)

Take me back!

Please take me back!!!

Take me back to the gift of life,

which started as an infant cry

acknowledging it's presence

in a whole new world,

a world it hasn't come to know.

Take me back to their elementary days

when their first school

was in their mother's space

when they wait for the stars

to hear their papa's tales

and their only pain

was not having enough play.

Take me back to adventure

when the infant is now a bigger picture

seeking a purpose for a meaningful life

and growing past sleeping to a gentle lullaby.

Take me back to curiosity

when a child wants to know everything

to differentiate between good and evil

a knowledge not treated too little.

Take me back to their obedient heart

when pleasure was taken

from hearing their parent talk

when the best times were made

in their parent's court

advice and counsels,

encouragement flux

Take me back to a chosen path

when the child has grown

to exercise their right

discreetly they thread

to make the right call

for fear that their image

and reputation might fall.

for their parents were their role model

and they listened to every word

without contempt.

will my children to me

be this close?

i hope to see,

i hope to know

Take Me Back (Part 6)

You felt my desire to go back,

back to when the world was stable,

stable in a perfectly imperfect way

that maintained peace in it's curious phase.

My words are not spoken

with uncertainty

that you ignore the curse

recent invention brings

praising evolution for changing

this generation's mentality

forgetting that one important

aspect of life is family.

oh no! this generation that I live in

we prefer showy display

of a fake life we seek

wasting time and currencies

on unnecessary flings

while to our families

we are a totally different being.

for shall i gain happiness

in praises from my friends?

friends who only hates

but laugh with me in pretense.

of what is loyalty

if not an unending oath

of true love and support

frequently shown?

Take me back

so that i may live

a life of nobility and loyalty

that i may hear

honest words of encouragement

that sooth my soul

just like nature's breath

There is no greater love

than from family,

because they sacrifice

for you remarkably.

drop the relative - for families

are not only bonded to you

by blood,

they are people who will stay with you

when everyone else runs.

The Generational Curse

There was, once told

A certain prophecy

that will travel through time

to the future -

A prophecy many ignore

written in Greek manuscript

A prophecy bound to happen

to this generation.

Woe to men

who acts in ignorance

as to the curse not known

to their youthful exuberance.

For men will be lovers of themselves,

lovers of money,

self-assuming and haughty.

Children will be disobedient to parents

and unthankful

not performing their duties

as they used to.

Loyalty will be an embarrassment

to someone who wishes to do right

and the mouth of blasphemers

will be quick to spit all the time.

Natural affection will be rare

and agreements will be broken.

You will be slandered

by words not meant to be spoken,

for there will be

no control

in the hearts of men

and absolute goodness will be far from them.

Their pleasure will be their god

and idolatry will be a norm.

What say you

to this dangerous curse?

It might be a prophecy

but must it have its accord?

Yes, many are words fulfilled

spoken in ancient tongues

but I bet you can escape

this generational curse.

CHAPTER FIVE

(The Escape)

The Escape

Hello.

Hi.

Crickets whispers at the background

was loud enough

to let them speak

but words fail.

For what will you say

to a known stranger?

A stranger you once called home,

A stranger that gives you

memories of a life

you once loved,

A stranger who is now cold.

If only there was a time machine

you would want to go back -

I know -

I've been there before.

To take back all those venom you spewed,

you wished it never happened

but what happened

to your emotions

that moment?

You were ready

to walk away

from all you've built at home

believing it was the best decision

you have ever made.

but you haven't made

any wise decision at all -

you just delayed

your right life

by using the wrong words

and forever will it be

engraved in their heart

like a sunburn

Yes! Life gives you

multiple choices

and you can always

start again from the last,

but can you erase

the stigma you inflicted

in the past?

Now you are back,

love outbound,

you've been away for long

and you crave

the love you had.

For every relationship

can be a success

if both parties

can sacrifice some pain.

This can be your lesson learned.

This can be your escape.

Always & Forever (Part 2)

Few years ago

we stood at this point

where I could die for you

for I was crazy in love.

I made an oath to you

to never give up -

little did we understand

life's cunning ploy.

We dived into the deep blue

and came out confused,

little or no experience

can rip you in twos.

What we experienced

can never be changed-

to know that love can

Stand any trial it face.

For an oath

I long to swear

to my damsel in distress,

that I may ease your mind a little

to the fear that camps your mettle.

If for fear I'll leave

makes you look pale,

then put it in my hands

and I will take your fear away.

For my leave will be

to take you with me

that where I am

you will be

with no discrepancy.

If you shed a tear

on my accord,

then I have failed you

and I do not deserve

to live at all.

But if your tear

was for a different account,

then that phase

will remember my name.

For my wrath will befall

your enemies

and my life's goal

will bring you happiness.

Let the sky of the heavens

hear me say,

my love for you is

forever this day.

We have made our mistakes

and from our mistakes

we have learned,

take me back to a better

life we've heard -

how we can be

better than our past years.

For vows are not to be broken

and memories not to be lost,

so I vow to keep your memory

forever in my lot.

How well did we find

our fairytale through tragic past,

but now I mean it

when I say I will

love you Always & Forever.

Epilogue: Marry My Fist

"You gambled away the money again, is that why you couldn't get me anything and proposed we go to a cheaper restaurant"? Lilith asked with a pitch in her tone expecting a different reply this time to temper her rising rage, well Gerald was indifferent about the situation as he replied; "but I got you flowers, I know how much you love tulips", raising his eyebrows continuously and smiling a one-sided smile to create a tempting offer with the hope of appearing as a gentleman and buying her smile. "These are not tulips you dummy", Lilith replied as she grabbed the flowers from his hands and flogged him with it. "And you just plucked them from my garden at our backyard when you came over, do you think I wouldn't recognize the flowers I am growing"? Lilith continued as she kept flogging him and expressing her anger, indicating the fact that he isn't doing it for the first time and it has become a habit. Gerald bending down trying to take cover, yet trying to ease the moment replied; "look at the brighter picture, the flower matches your velvet skirt, everyone in the restaurant will be looking at you babe, and that is a very beautiful garden you are growing at our backyard, but how do you manage to maintain its beauty for this long and still have another favorite flower"?

Gerald was scrupulously trying to understand his wife's enthusiasm in liking one flower but growing another. It has been a constant challenge in their five years of marriage as Lilith complains about Gerald's incapability of paying attention to the little details that ignites her emotional excitement. On the contrary, Gerald considers himself free and satisfying in the game called life. Has he made mistakes in the past? A billion. Does he dwell on his mistakes? Not at all. Does he make changes? In his own way, yes. He and Lilith has been together since fresh year in college and they married just immediately after graduation.

 "Tulips are hard to find here that's why I grow roses, fool" Lilith screamed. "If they are so hard to find why do you expect me to keep bringing them"? Gerald reverts. "Because you are the man, idiot, you do hard things for love," Lilith shouted. "Well it isn't easy being with you", Gerald said in a low tone as he took out pieces of flowers from his body watching Lilith storm off in anger with her hand bag after flogging him with the flowers he got her from her garden. "I will get you tulips on our next date babe", he shouted enough for Lilith to hear him from a distance, "you know I don't like you being mad at me, we will talk about it when I return, but for now I will be going to eat because I am hungry." Lilith shouted from afar; "you better not eat that food without me, make sure you bring it home or you will be sleeping in the dogs kernel tonight," then she turned back and walked back home.

About the Author

DAVIDSON REHAM is a respected poet, designer, entrepreneur, and the founder of an online technology company that provides technical services to organizations and individuals alike.

His love for art and design is widely recognized from his conversations, goals, attitudes and works. He set out to building a community of technocrats in the eastern part of Nigeria and still strategize to extend that vision all through Africa.

Davidson comes from a family of five consisting of more women which actually exposed him to deep knowledge of how women thinks – helping him to compare, contrast, and connects the reasoning of both the male and female gender. This brought him to an understanding of what is essential to the creation of meaningful connection and a happier life.

Davidson is known by his contemporaries for his creativity, critical thinking, principles and introverted lifestyle. His skill pushed him to help people with some of the knowledge he has acquired especially in topics like: Art, tech, mental health, life, religion and so on – therefore the creation of this book and many more to come.

Davidson's goal is centered on spreading knowledge, love and practicing exactly what he preaches as he believes that change can only start with he who request it.

Coming soon from Davidson Reham

In a world where love is ignored,

Strife is promoted

wrecking havoc

and damaging sanity.

Mentality has changed

and health has walked out the door,

taking young lives on a long vacation

to a dream world of no return.

Who will tell them

how to survive?

How to stay sane

In a world of insanity?

How to converse

with life's unexpected visitors?

How to recognize those visitors?

"Going Mental" will tell you how.

The ultimate guide

to a better mental health.

Anticipate!!!

www.ingramcontent.com/pod-product-compliance
Lightning Source LLC
Chambersburg PA
CBHW061331120726
48001CB00002B/789